NATURAL SCIENCE 1

1 MOVE YOUR BODY!

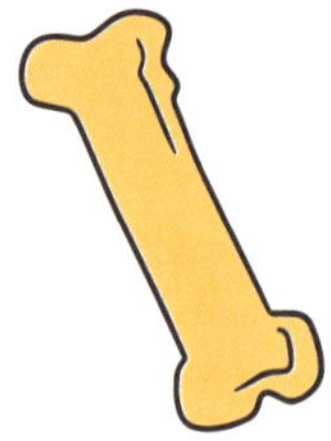

1 Match.

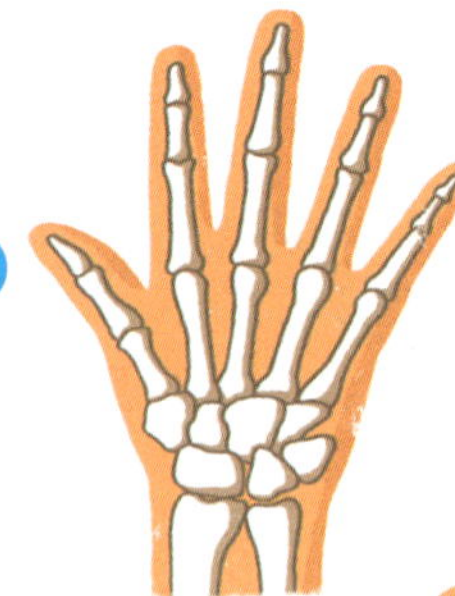

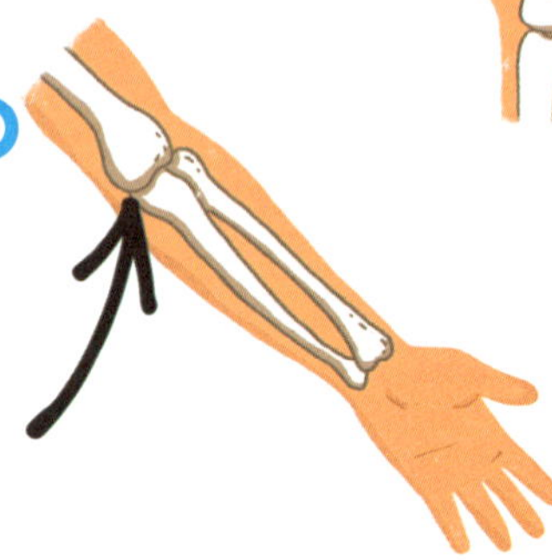

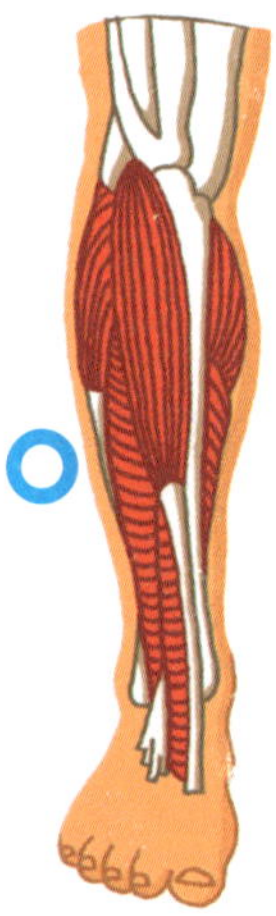

a joint

b bones

c muscles

2 Find the words.

shoulder elbow ~~wrist~~ hip knee ankle

s	y	h	p	w	v	k	y	o
s	h	d	p	e	l	b	o	w
a	u	o	x	j	c	n	l	r
n	v	f	u	d	h	b	s	i
k	g	n	x	l	d	k	z	s
l	g	h	h	j	d	n	r	t
e	t	k	l	l	o	e	a	e
w	t	h	i	p	i	e	r	l
q	p	r	r	e	w	m	g	a

3 Colour the head, torso and limbs.

4 Write *true* or *false*.

a My arms and legs are limbs. true false

b My ears are part of my limbs. true false

c My tummy is part of my torso. true false

d My eyes are in my head. true false

5 Complete the sentences with the correct number.

a I have got __two__ eyes.

b I have got ________ nose.

c I have got ________ tongue.

d I have got ________ ears.

e I have got ________ mouth.

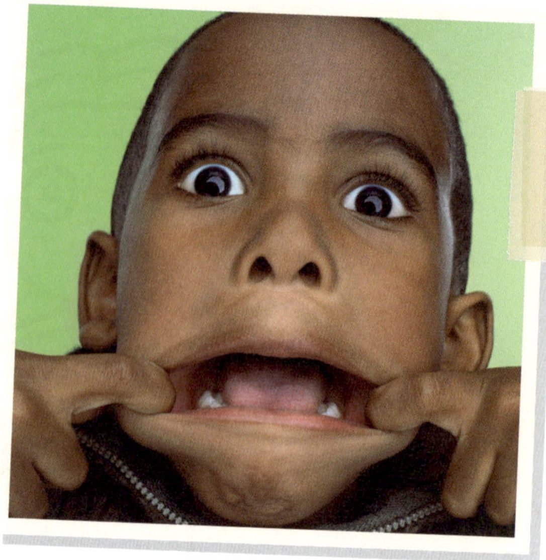

6 Look at the pictures. Look at the letters. Write the words.

a 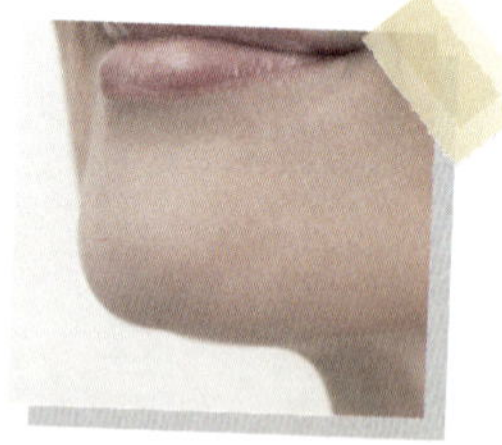 __c__ __h__ __i__ __n__ h n i c

b 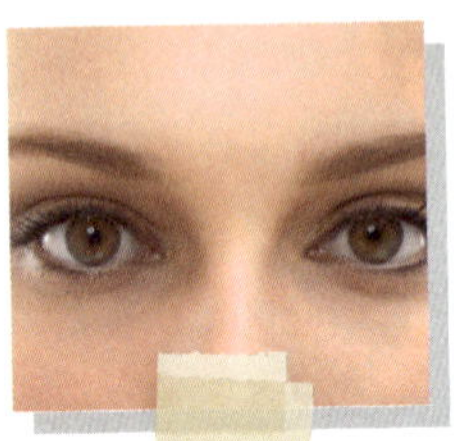 __ __ __ __ s y e e

c 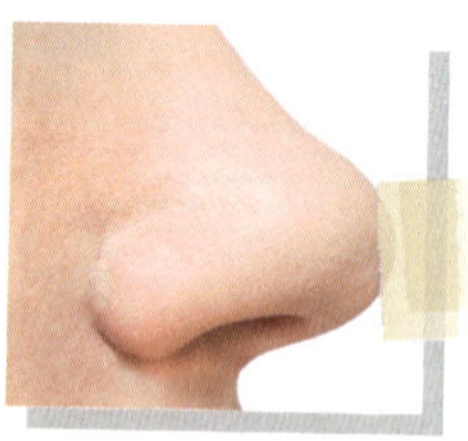 __ __ __ __ e s n o

d 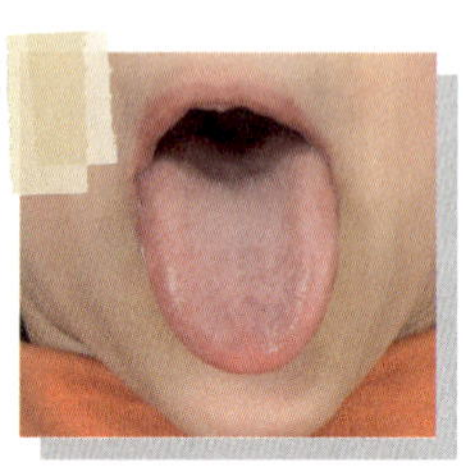 __ __ __ __ __ __ n t o g e u

e 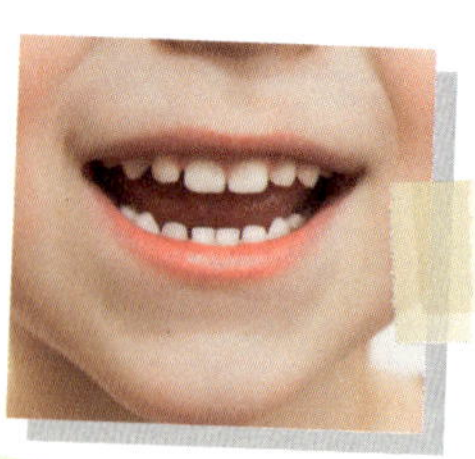 __ __ __ __ __ h u t m o

7 Read and draw the alien. Colour.

My alien has got three eyes and five ears.
My alien has got red cheeks and a purple nose.

8 Trace the words. Colour these parts of the body.

hands

feet

tummy

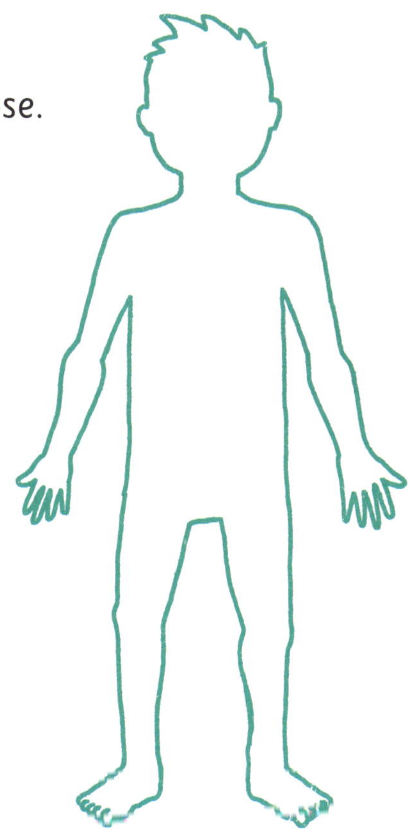

9 Look and read. Put a tick (✓) or a cross (✗) in the box.

a  This is a foot. [✓]

b  This is a finger. [ ]

c  This is a knee. [ ]

d 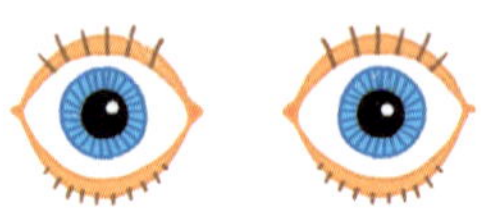 This is a toe. [ ]

e 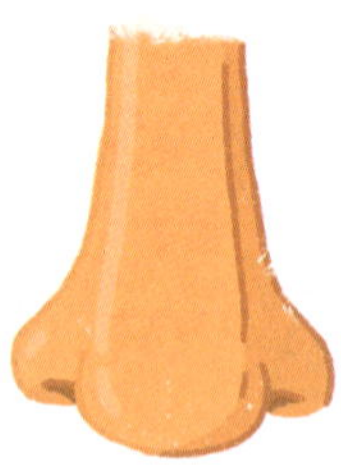 This is a tongue. [ ]

10 Circle the correct option.

a *Joints* / *Bones* help you move.

b Your tummy is in your *head* / *torso*.

11 Match the photos to the correct sense.

see · smell · taste · touch · hear

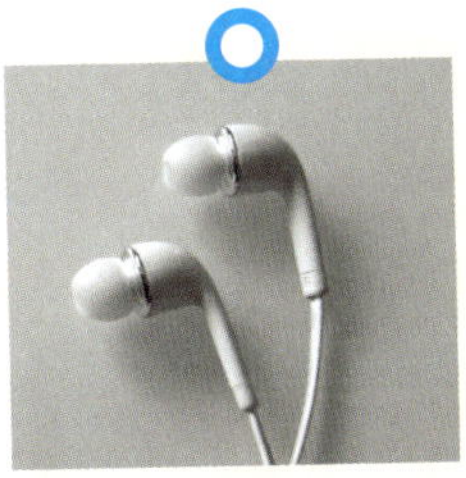

12 Look and write.

~~touch~~ hear smell taste

a  touch

b  ________

c  ________

d  ________

13 Complete the sentences.

ears hands nose ~~eyes~~

a I see with my eyes .

b I smell with my ________ .

c I touch with my ________ .

d I hear with my ________ .

2 STAY STRONG, LIVE LONG!

1 Match.

carbohydrates

proteins

fats

fruit and vegetables

dairy

2 Circle *fruit* or *vegetable*.

a

fruit / vegetable

b

fruit / vegetable

c

fruit / vegetable

d

fruit / vegetable

3 Circle the odd one out.

fruit and vegetables

carbohydrates

proteins

dairy

fats

4 Trace and match.

proteins

carbohydrates

fruit and vegetables

dairy

fats

5 Are these snacks healthy? Put a tick (✓) or a cross (✗) in the box.

a donut

☒ ✗

b pear

☐

c crisps

☐

d cola

☐

e yoghurt

☐

f chocolate

☐

6 Draw your favourite healthy snack. Complete the sentence.

My favourite healthy snack is ____________________.

7 Look at the pictures. Look at the letters. Write the words.

a  b r e a k f a s t — r e s b a f t a k

b  _ _ _ _ _ — s n a k c

c  _ _ _ _ _ — u n c h l

d  _ _ _ _ _ _ — i d n n r e

8 Circle the correct option.

a Eat *three* / *four* / *five* times a day.

b Eat five portions of *fruit and vegetables* / *dairy* / *fats* a day.

9 Colour.

healthy unhealthy

a 

b 

c 

d 

10 Circle the correct spelling. Write the words under the pictures.

muscles mussles	healty healthy	heart hart

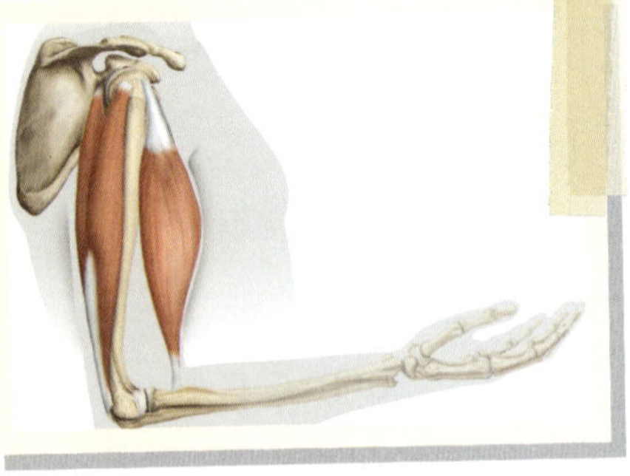

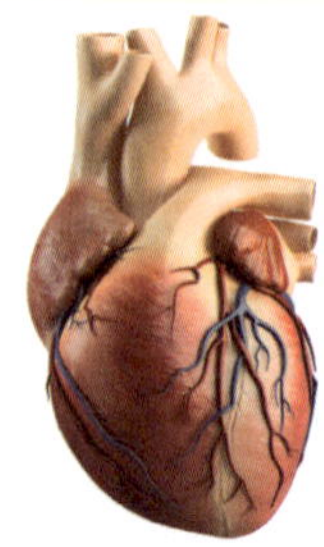

______ ______ ______

11 Circle the correct word.

a I brush my *teeth* / *tongue* after meals.

b I have a shower every *week* / *day*.

c I wash my *hands* / *hair* before meals.

12 Match.

1 

2 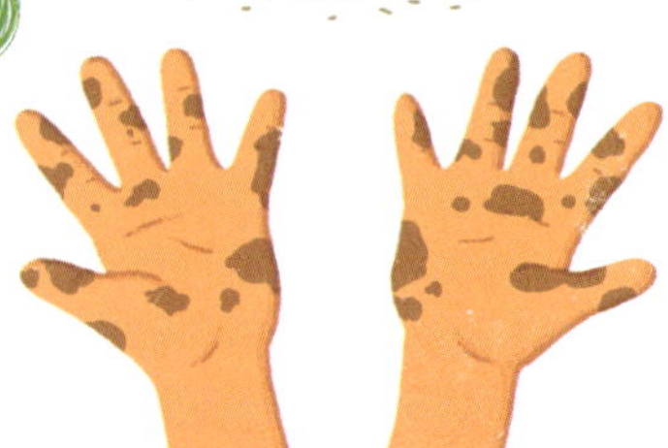

a 

b 

13 **Read about Little Pasteur. Choose a word from the box. Write the correct word next to letters b–d.**

school

~~crisps~~

sandwiches

yoghurt

I don't like (a) crisps . They are unhealthy.
I always bring healthy snacks to (b) ____________.
I like fruit, carrots, cereal, (c) ____________ and
(d) ____________.

14 **How do they feel? Write.**

happy angry sad

a

____

b

____

c

____

3 ANIMAL PLANET

1 Match.

a 

b 

c 

d 

farm

ocean

the Arctic

forest

2 Circle the odd one out.

invertebrates

vertebrates

3 Look and read. Put a tick (✓) or a cross (✗) in the box.

a This is a prawn. It is an invertebrate. ☑ ✓

b This is a jellyfish. It is an invertebrate. ☐

c This is a dolphin. It is a vertebrate. ☐

d This is a starfish. It is an invertebrate. ☐

4 Draw your favourite vertebrate and invertebrate. Complete the sentences.

My favourite vertebrate is

_______________________ .

My favourite invertebrate is

_______________________ .

5 **How do these animals move? Write.**

swim slither ~~walk~~ fly

a 

b 

c 

d 

a walk ________ b ________ c ________ d ________

6 **Draw the animals from Activity 5 in the correct place.**

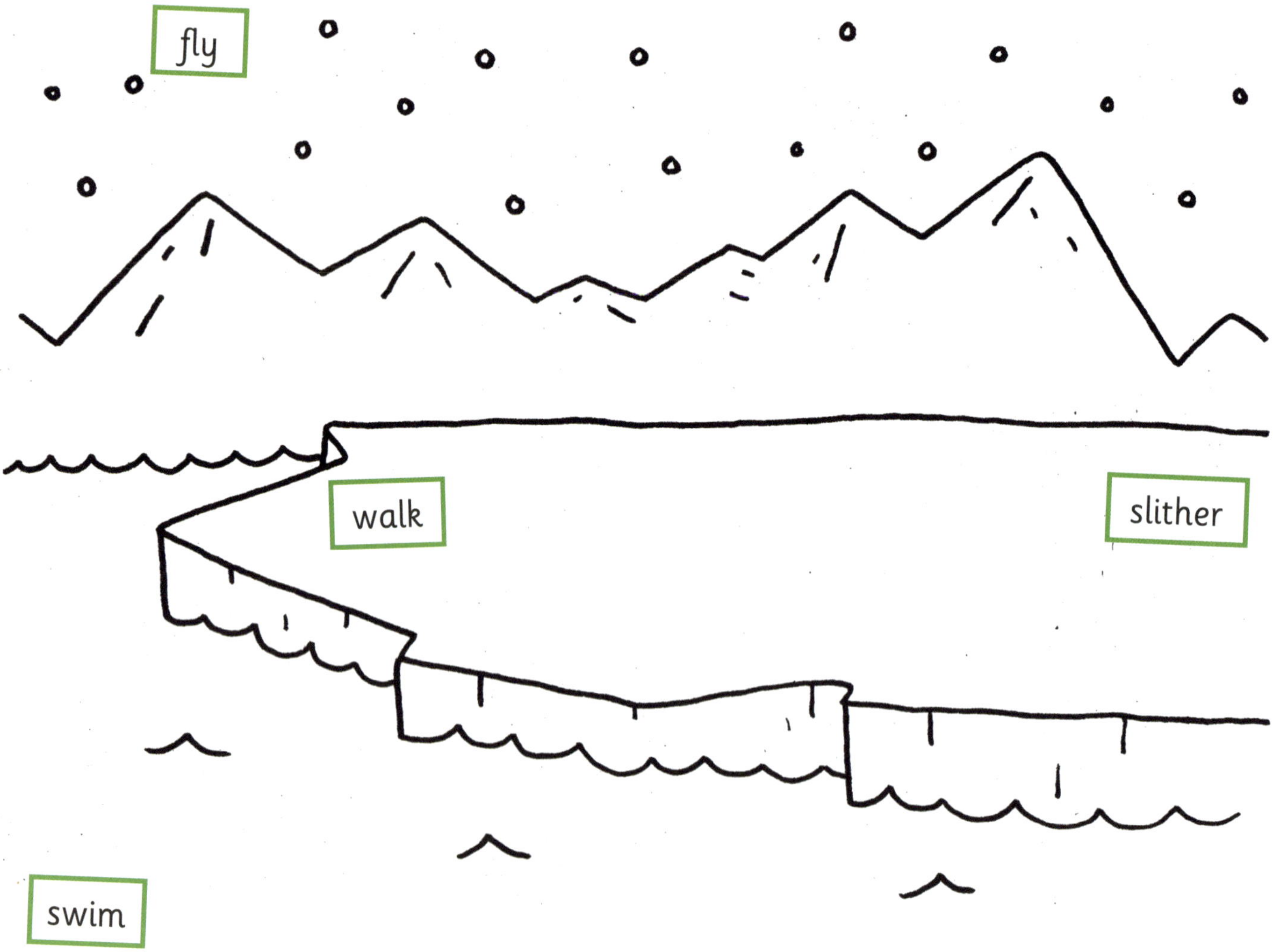

7 Look at the pictures. Look at the letters. Write the words.

a 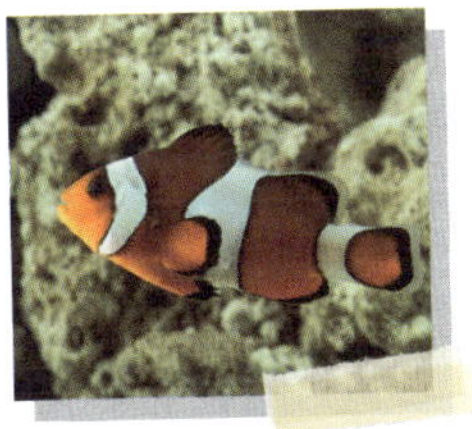 f i s h — letters: s, i, h, f

b  __ __ __ __ — letters: d, b, i, r

c  __ __ __ __ __ __ __ — letters: e, l, i, r, p, e, t

d  __ __ __ __ __ __ — letters: l, m, a, a, m, m

e  __ __ __ __ __ __ __ __ __ — letters: h, b, i, p, a, n, a, i, m

8 Colour the mammals yellow and the amphibians blue.

9 Circle the odd one out.

mammal 

reptile 

bird 

amphibian 

fish 

10 Where do these animals live? Write.

~~badger~~ cow sheep hen owl fox

Wild	Domestic
badger	

11 Choose a word from the box.
Write the correct word next to letters b–d.

Hello! I am a rainbow lorikeet and I am very colourful. I am a (**a**) ___bird___ and I can fly.

I live in the (**b**) ______________ and I can see lots of (**c**) ______________ .

(**d**) ______________, snakes and frogs are my neighbours.

birds

rainforest

trees

koalas

12 Look at the photo. Circle the correct option.

a It is a *vertebrate* / *invertebrate*.

b It can *fly* / *swim* / *slither* / *walk*.

c It is a *mammal* / *reptile* / *fish* / *bird* / *amphibian*.

d It *has got* / *has not got* any legs.

4 FLOWER POWER!

1 Look and write.

stem seeds flower leaves ~~roots~~

a 

roots

b 

____

c 

____

d 

____

e 

____

2 Label the daisy.

flower stem leaves roots

a ________________

b ________________

c ________________

d ________________

3 Look and read. Put a tick (✓) or a cross (✗) in the box.

a A tree is a bush.  [✗]

b Bushes have woody stems.  [ ]

c Trees have not got any branches.  [ ]

d Wheat is grass.  [ ]

e A round bush is a tree.  [ ]

4 Complete the sentences.

bushes grass ~~trunk~~ branches

Trees are tall. They have a thick (**a**) trunk and (**b**) ____________ .
(**c**) ____________ have got a lot of woody stems.
(**d**) ____________ is bendy.

5 Colour the cultivated plants green.

a 

b 

c 

d 

6 Look and read. Write *yes* or *no*.

a There is a farmer working on the farm. yes

b There are three hens. ________

c There are cultivated plants. ________

d The cultivated plants are lettuce, oranges and dandelions. ________

e There are some wild flowers. ________

7 What do we use these plants for? Label the pictures.

food medicine clothes ~~furniture~~

a 

b 

c 

d 

a furniture

b __________

c __________

d __________

8 Match.

a 

b 

c 

d 

strawberry

cotton

pine tree

chamomile

9 What do plants need? Put a tick (✓) in the correct boxes.

a  ☑

b  ☐

c  ☐

d 

☐

e  ☐

10 Write *true* or *false*.

a Plants need water to live. true false

b Plants need air to live. true false

c Plants can live in drawers. true false

d Plants need orange juice. true false

11 Which photos show children respecting plants? Put a tick (✓) in the correct boxes.

12 Colour the bad behaviour red and the good behaviour green.

5 I'M ALIVE!

1 Look and write.

animal people plants

a

____

b

____

c

____

2 Order the life cycle of a plant. Write numbers 1–4 in the boxes.

Plants grow.

☐

Plants die.

☐

Plants reproduce.

☐

Plants are born.

1

3 What do animals and people need to live? Draw.

______ ______ ______

4 Write *yes* or *no*.

a Plants need milk to live. no

b People, animals and plants need food to live. ______

c People, animals and plants need air to live. ______

d Animals need clothes to live. ______

5 Number the pictures and trace the words.

Animals ...

a

reproduce.

b

are born.

c

grow.

6 Complete the sentences.

babies girl boy born reproduce adults

First, people are born and they are (**a**) babies . Then, they grow into a (**b**) ________ or a (**c**) ________ . They continue growing and become (**d**) ________ . They (**e**) ________ and have babies.

7 Circle the odd one out.

living things

non-living things

8 Circle the words.

reproducegrowbornairwaterfood

9 Look and read. Put a tick (✓) or a cross (✗) in the box.

a This is a living thing. ☑

b This is a living thing. ☐

c This is a non-living thing. ☐

d This is a non-living thing. ☐

e These are non-living things. ☐

10 Complete the sentences.

living air water non-living ~~lion~~

A ___lion___ is a ______________ thing because it needs ______________ , food and ______________ to live.

11 What is it? Read and write the answer.

a chair

a gorilla

the sun

a sunflower

a

It is a non-living thing.
It gives you heat and light.
It is yellow.
You can see it in the sky.
What is it?
It is ______________________ .

b

It is a non-living thing.
It is made of wood.
It has got four legs.
You sit on it.
What is it?
It is ______________________ .

12 Find the words.

cloud ~~sun~~ rock water sand

s	a	n	d	q	a	w
c	o	y	b	w	r	a
b	l	t	e	x	o	t
j	m	o	s	f	c	e
r	u	s	u	n	k	r
a	q	p	c	d	y	o

13 **Colour the living things green. Colour the non-living things red.**

14 **Look at the picture in Activity 13 again and read the questions. Write one-word answers.**

a How many people are in the canoe? __________

b What is the man doing? he is __________

c How many tents are there? __________

15 **Draw a living thing.**

6 FEELINGS LAB

1 Match.

a

b

c

- I can help.
- I am nice.
- I am clever.

2 Circle the odd one out.

good choices at school

good choices at home

3 **Look at the pictures and read the questions. Write one-word answers.**

a Where are they? in the kitchen

b What is the mum putting in the fridge? ____________

c Is the girl helping? ____________

d Is the boy being kind to the girl? ____________

e Is the girl happy? ____________

4 **Circle the super classmates.**

a

b

c

d

5 Look at the pictures. Write the good choices in the table.

With friends	At school	At home
play fair		

play fair

get your schoolbag ready

listen to others

be kind

6 Draw examples of good behaviour at school, at home and with your friends.

7 Choose a word from the box. Write the correct word next to letters b–e.

To be a good (**a**) friend you have to (**b**) __________ fair!
Always use kind (**c**) __________: *please* and *thank you* are the magic words.
Never be a (**d**) __________ and take care of (**e**) __________ __________ .

bully

fair

~~friend~~

words

little ones

play

8 Draw a friend. Complete the sentences.

kind   fair   thank you   helps

Name: ________________
My friend is ________________ and plays ________________ .
My friend ________________ me.
My friend always says ________________ .

9 How do you help at home? Tick (✓) or cross (✗).

a I make my bed ✓
b I fight with my brothers or sisters. ☐
c I get my schoolbag ready. ☐
d I tidy my room. ☐
e I keep calm. ☐

10 Colour the good choices in the picture.

11 Find the words.

listen help share respect

l	j	s	h	a	r	e
l	i	f	b	m	p	g
r	e	s	p	e	c	t
n	e	e	t	v	y	c
d	s	f	h	e	l	p
z	i	a	y	p	n	m

HOW DO YOU SAY ...?

Try writing these words in your own language!

Unit 1 – Move your body!

bones ______________________
joints ______________________
muscles ______________________
limbs ______________________
torso ______________________
hear ______________________
taste ______________________
touch ______________________
see ______________________
smell ______________________

Unit 2 – Stay strong, live long!

dairy ______________________
fats ______________________
fruit ______________________
vegetables ______________________
carbohydrates ______________________
proteins ______________________
breakfast ______________________
snack ______________________
lunch ______________________
dinner ______________________
healthy ______________________
unhealthy ______________________

Unit 3 – Animal planet

invertebrate ______________________________
vertebrate ______________________________
fly ______________________________
slither ______________________________
swim ______________________________
walk ______________________________
amphibian ______________________________
bird ______________________________
fish ______________________________
mammal ______________________________
reptile ______________________________

Unit 4 – Flower power!

flower ______________________________
leaves ______________________________
roots ______________________________
seeds ______________________________
stem ______________________________
bush ______________________________
branch ______________________________
grass ______________________________
tree ______________________________
trunk ______________________________
cultivated ______________________________
wild ______________________________

Unit 5 – I'm alive!

be born ______________________

die ______________________

grow ______________________

reproduce ______________________

air ______________________

food ______________________

light ______________________

water ______________________

living ______________________

non-living ______________________

Unit 6 – Feelings lab

be kind ______________________

be nice ______________________

help ______________________

be honest ______________________

keep calm ______________________

listen ______________________

respect ______________________

tidy up ______________________

try your best ______________________

work hard ______________________